Citizens of Peace

Abhijit Naskar is the twenty-first century mind of science, whose gentle and glorious philosophical touch has enabled modern Neuroscience to effectively engage in the human society towards diminishing the ever-growing conflicts among religions. As an untiring advocate of global harmony and peace, he became a beloved best-selling author all over the world with his very first book "The Art of Neuroscience in Everything". With various of his pioneering ventures into the Neuropsychology of religious sentiments, he has hugely contributed in the eradication of religious differences in our world, for which he is popularly hailed as a humanitarian neuroscientist, who takes the human civilization in the path of sweet general harmony.

CITIZENS OF
PEACE

BEYOND THE SAVAGERY
OF SOVEREIGNTY

ABHIJIT NASKAR

Also by Abhijit Naskar

The Art of Neuroscience in Everything
Your Own Neuron: A Tour of Your Psychic Brain
The God Parasite: Revelation of Neuroscience
The Spirituality Engine
Love Sutra: The Neuroscientific Manual of Love
Homo: A Brief History of Consciousness
Neurosutra: The Abhijit Naskar Collection
Autobiography of God: Biopsy of A Cognitive Reality
Biopsy of Religions: Neuroanalysis towards Universal
Tolerance
Prescription: Treating India's Soul
What is Mind?
In Search of Divinity: Journey to The Kingdom of Conscience
Love, God & Neurons: Memoir of a scientist who found
himself by getting lost
The Islamophobic Civilization: Voyage of Acceptance
Neurons of Jesus: Mind of A Teacher, Spouse & Thinker
Neurons, Oxygen & Nanak
The Education Decree
Principia Humanitas
The Krishna Cancer
Rowdy Buddha: The First Sapiens
We Are All Black: A Treatise on Racism
The Bengal Tigress: A Treatise on Gender Equality
Either Civilized or Phobic: A Treatise on Homosexuality
Wise Mating: A Treatise on Monogamy
Illusion of Religion: A Treatise on Religious
Fundamentalism
The Film Testament
Human Making is Our Mission: A Treatise on Parenting
I Am The Thread: My Mission
7 Billion Gods: Humans Above All
Lord is My Sheep: Gospel of Human
Morality Absolute
A Push in Perception
Let The Poor Be Your God
Conscience over Nonsense
Saint of The Sapiens
Time to Save Medicine
Fabric of Humanity

Build Bridges not Walls: In the name of Americana
The Constitution of The United Peoples of Earth
Lives to Serve Before I Sleep
When Humans Unite: Making A World Without Borders
All For Acceptance
Mission Reality

This is My Offering to My
Homeland Earth,
with the hope that one day soon,
all my sisters and brothers will
stand as one.

CONTENTS

The Earth Anthem 1

A Sense of Universal Community 7

Either Sovereignty or Serenity 21

Rise, O Patriots of The Planet! 31

BIBLIOGRAPHY 65

The Earth Anthem

The Planetary Anthem of Earth

O My Mother Earth,
I am your stubborn child,
I may fall again and again,
Rising right back up I smile.
I come from different religions,
Different colors though my skin reflects,
At heart I am one o mother,
At heart I am beyond all sects.

O My Mother Earth,
Never turn your back on me,
I may be arrogant sometimes,
But I always need thee.
I'm full of pride rather often,
Often I'm blind to necessities,
But fret not o my loving mother,
Sooner or later I realize my atrocities.

O My Mother Earth,
I may act greedy sometimes,
But if my neighbors are in pain,

To help them my heart chimes.
I make mistakes o mother,
And that too quite often,
But even the scorching sun,
Can't make my zeal disheartened.

O My Mother Earth,
I may or may not have riches,
But I am not poor my dear,
For I have compassion that never glitches.
You have given me all,
All that I'll ever need,
With it I'll win the universe,
And to my agonies I'll pay no heed.

O My Mother Earth,
You've given me tongues many,
But I promise to not let languages,
Cause in your home disharmony.
Love has no gender,
Compassion has no religion,
Character has no race,
In acceptance I seek salvation.

O My Mother Earth,
I am your stubborn child,
I may fall again and again,
Rising right back up I smile.

A Sense of Universal Community

Time - time is the most fascinating and most remarkable measure of all - it's on the basis of time that we make all our observations in existence. Hence, though the psychological line of time is rather nonexistent outside human memory, it is nevertheless of peerless significance. It's significant because it gives us a perspective of where we have been, where we are, and in which direction we are going.

Time brings evolution into perspective - into human perspective. And we do that, based on solely our memories, but those very memories manifest themselves in the form of time. In short, time is memory - where there is memory, there is time, where there is no memory, there is no time.

But what is the use of such time, if we don't bring it to use in mending our errors, in mending the mistakes our previous generations committed, either due to lack of understanding or due to absolute primitiveness.

In the wild kingdom, lack of understanding and primitiveness go hand in hand, but as humans became smart enough to build civilizations, we get to observe the ignorance and primitiveness getting separated. For example, in the so-called modern society of today, a man may have the intricate understanding of the workings of the atoms, but at the same time, he may be primitive still to look down on lay people. In the old days, our primitiveness kept us alive in the jungle, but today it acts as nothing but the proof of our animal nature.

And this very primitiveness that we have inherited from our uncivilized and wild animal ancestors, still dominates many aspects of the functionings of the modern society, however in most cases, it masquerades itself as pompous and apparently civilized ideologies. Hence, most of the human population takes pride in those ideologies, without knowing their practical implications in a global society such as ours.

Externally we may have become advanced enough to dream of colonizing Mars in a not so distant future, but internally, the ideologies that keep running the human population here on earth, have remained the same over the past few millennia. The labels and the outward characteristics of those ideologies may have changed, but their practical traits remain the same.

For example, dictatorship has had an external makeover and is labeled today as democracy, where the people are kept under control by means of false security. And in this new dictatorship, people are happy as long as they are made to think that they themselves are making the decisions of their life, while in reality those decisions are made under the dictatorship of specific political parties that mainly consist of politicians, who in most cases have no more brains than termites. And this process of social delusion is sustained by the modern con-artists (either conscious or subconscious) called politicians (not all) with the use of psychologically reinforcing terms such as "democracy", "freedom", "sovereignty" and many more.

In the hands of these savage and meritless swindlers, patriotism is the most potent weapon to manipulate the minds of the gullible public. Feed them a few lies encapsulated in patriotism and they will not mind electing even a pompous and megalomaniacal bully as their representative.

Sovereignty is a delusion, and the most dangerous delusion at that, as far as peacemaking is concerned. Blind pursuit of sovereignty only brings destruction upon the world. In principle, sovereignty means self-reliance, but in practice it turns into blind pursuit of power and authority, often at the price of discrimination and segregation.

In actuality, there is no such thing as "our own country", because no country belongs to us, no land belongs to us. Most humans are refugees in our countries because all our ancestors scattered across the globe from our homeland Africa. Even the Motherland Africa doesn't belong to us, we belong to Africa. The world doesn't belong to us, we belong to the world.

Therefore, sovereignty can be the trait of an amateur non-global species, but for humankind to be hailed as true sapiens, all pursuit of exclusive power and authority must be renounced and all the powers in our veins must be brought out to solve the issues that torment human life anywhere in the world.

If you are to be a civilized and conscientious human, you no longer have the luxury to think that troubles of people in others countries are none of your business. For peace and progress to shower on humankind, we must extend the boundaries of our family, from our immediate family to our neighbors and then to our whole world. If we the humans don't have the sense of sovereignty of the whole world, then it's no sovereignty of a civilized species, because every other form of national sovereignty is only glorified tribalism.

However, fact of the matter is, tribalism still runs through our nerves in the form of primitive instinct, but since we do not like to admit that we are primitives, we have devised new and pompous terms for that tribalism, such as sovereignty and nationalism. And people are made to believe by their socio-cultural convention that sovereignty and nationalism are of utmost importance. However, I am sorry to say that, they may have been important in the past for our ancestors, but they are no longer important, in fact, they are downright dangerous.

To put it simply, sovereignty is injurious to humankind. We can either have sovereignty or harmony, not both - we can either have sovereignty or universal acceptance, not both - we can either have sovereignty or humanity, not both. As long as we think in terms of sovereign nations, we can never have a serene planet. Sovereignty and serenity can't go hand in hand.

Throw away all sovereignty and rise with universal responsibility – with a sense of universal community. Love the humans across the globe, only then can you hope to give a beautiful planet to your children. Hug everyone, love everyone - that's the only tradition that can stop the fall of humankind.

And to the so-called realists I say, fret not, I am not talking about some utopian realm, where there will be no differences among people, rather what I am pointing out is that, to have a world free from war and lethal conflicts, the nations must stop feeling, thinking and behaving like purely separate lands on earth, instead they should feel, think and behave as belonging to the grand country called earth. And to achieve this, all separations must first be erased from the human heart, once it's done, peace, harmony and unity will slowly begin to manifest on earth quite automatically.

Savages chase sovereignty, saints chase unity. The reason that the world still needs to worry about wars, is because its leaders are more interested in national security than global security. Now, let's go slow here, because the situation is rather complex. One may most intellectually proclaim, global security can only be attained through national security.

However, in reality, the very term security here is the root of all national and global insecurities. The urge for absolute security within an imaginary border, compels the primitive minds to act like tribal nationalists, which in turn, turns nation against nation. No nationalism can ever bring peace and harmony and global upliftment in the world, because nationalism is innately biased towards the wellbeing of the people of one nation, even if it means sacrificing the wellbeing of the people of another nation.

Think about the cold wars going on right now around the world, between neighboring nations, such as between America and Russia, between England and France, between India and Pakistan, and so on. It's called cold because, "war" is too primitive a term for the so-called civilized humans to be a part of officially, so they add a term "cold" to it and keep the fire of war between nations burning in their heart. So, on the outside, they pretend to be civilized, progressive and free from the traits of warmongering, but inside, they are as dumb, primitive and tribal as our ancestors once were in the jungle. And so long as we have any such thing as "my nation" and "your nation", we'll not have "our world", because, to have "our world", we must first give up our tribalistic loyalty to any one nation.

In a war, both sides genuinely believe that they are on the side of righteousness, yet no righteousness ever shows them the futility of the very war they are fighting. Because, both sides are driven by the instinctual force of nationalist patriotism. So, think of the countless wars that have caused gallons and gallons of bloodshed, all because warriors on both sides were incapable of reasoning due to the cognitive blindness caused by nationalism or patriotism (in the conventional sense).

In practice, patriotism and nationalism are basically one and the same thing. Both these terms are formed in the society on the foundation of the evolutionary psychological element of group-loyalty. The bases for group loyalty, which in this case is national loyalty, are lodged in human needs of wellbeing and survival of the group. At the level of the nation, the group fulfills economic, sociocultural, and political needs, giving individuals a sense of security, a feeling of belonging, and prestige. While these needs are regarded as universal, their strength appears to vary in different nations and in different individuals. And this variation determines the level of patriotism from person to person.

The group loyalty phenomenon is largely a product of the brain's subconscious instinctual drives, quite like libido, and that is why it may ensure the wellbeing and survival of the group but on its own it also fosters negative attitude towards out-group members. Let's concoct a thought experiment to elaborate this matter further.

Say some people are dancing in a club. Among them are three youngsters. Two of them are boyfriend and girlfriend and the third one is a drunk pervert. Now imagine that the drunk youngster misbehaves with the girlfriend of another person and in order to protect her dignity the boyfriend blows a punch right over the drunkard's nose. With a bleeding nose the youngster reaches his dorm where he lives with his fellow dorm mates. Seeing him bleeding all the boys in the dorm without even thinking, act like loyal friends and march ahead to confront the boyfriend. There they engage in a bloody battle with the boyfriend who happens to be a Tai Chi expert and all the dorm mates end up in the hospital with broken bones. Here, only if the dorm mates had used their faculty of reasoning and tried to understand the context in which their fellow youngster had been punched, they would not only have avoided a dangerous consequence, but also they could have realized that the real fault was in their friend's behavior.

Blind nationalism is as dangerous as religious fundamentalism. In religious fundamentalism deluded pests driven by their false perception of religion hail themselves to be the only religious people on earth and disregard all other religions as false and inferior. Likewise, in nationalist fundamentalism traditional bigots driven by their supremacist ego hail their own nation to be the greatest and belittle all other nations as lesser society, either explicitly or implicitly.

Great evils have been carried out in the name of religion and nation, all because people driven by the raw sentiment of group-loyalty lose their humanity.

Nationalism or patriotism has been an effective instinctual force in the survival of a group of people, especially when our ancestors lived amidst wild animals. Their patriotism towards their tribe kept them strong and united as a tribe, which increased their chances of survival against attacks from predators and invasions of other tribes. And that's why it's so damn difficult till this day to not feel patriotic (which mostly includes goose bumps and an overflow of emotions) when you listen to a patriotic song or watch a patriotic movie.

Reason has no bearing over patriotism, for it's all about feeling. Sentiments or emotional drives know no reason. For example, if a naked lady comes and stands in front of a young man, it is biologically impossible for the man to not feel aroused, likewise, when you meet a person from your native land, while roaming in another country, it's impossible for you to not feel a sense of closeness to that person.

However, the time has arisen that we begin to foster the same kind of closeness with every human on earth, regardless of whether they belong to our native land or our native tongue or our native religion and so on. Now is the time that patriotism gains a wider and more inclusive meaning in the collective psyche of the human species. Now is the time that every human on earth becomes patriotic, not towards his or her nation, but towards the entire humankind.

Either Sovereignty or Serenity

Patriotism is an autopilot mechanism, just like sexuality. And these autopilot mechanisms are what we call instincts. And they are there in our genetic blueprint in order to ensure that our kind survives across time, even without the intervention of the conscious mind. And in this process of survival so far, reasoning has played very little part, if any.

But things have begun to change for us humans recently in the last few thousand years, when we severed the umbilical cord connecting us to nature. Rest of the animal kingdom, excluding us humans, have to still rely on their instincts, as they remain at the mercy of nature, but we the humans have become intelligent enough to not rely on instincts and fight nature to survive.

Despite all our external advancements, internally we have remained the same old apes that once roamed the savanna of Africa. In an attempt to make life comfortable, what we are really doing is, caring mostly for our instinctual survival needs, not unlike wild animals - the only difference is that, we have developed clothing and ascetic amenities to cover up our external primitiveness, but no innovation has allowed us to cover up our internal primitiveness.

And no innovation will ever be able to help us be in control of our internal forces without ruining our psychological stability. So, to conquer our internal primitiveness, we have to rely on our mind apparatus - we have to rely on our conscience - we have to rely on our morality - we have to rely on our sense of righteousness, original righteousness, not the phony socially conditioned righteousness.

But the point is, no faculty of our mind is constant, they are all evolving - they are all growing - and as a result, we as sentient beings are always growing. So, even our sense of conscience or morality or righteousness can lead us astray sometimes - away from the path of truth, liberty and equality - so we must always be conscious of our very faculty of conscience - we must be aware of whether we have let our instincts keep our conscience stagnant without us being aware of it - we must at all times be aware of our sense of righteousness - we must at all times be aware of our very capacity of awareness.

The only reason wars and conflicts still prevail in this world is because we are not aware - we are not aware of our thoughts - we are not aware of our behaviors - we are not aware of our emotions - most of our thoughts, emotions and behaviors are dictated by our instinctual autopilot mechanisms. Most of our morality is instinctual, most of our righteousness is instinctual, most of our acts of conscience are instinctual. In short, most of our civilized behavior is instinctually dictated, rather than being driven by a genuine sense of civilization.

People from one side of the border most proudly kill people from the other side of the border and they call it patriotism. If this is patriotism, then I'd rather be the most unpatriotic person on earth, than be a savage patriot with no more brains in the skull than a neanderthal. Whom are you fighting, who are your enemies, and on whose orders are you fighting them, and how much sure are you that the superiors and their political authorities who are giving you all those commands, are actually even capable of making decisions on matters of peace and progress!

Being a politician, doesn't mean being capable of making the best decisions for a people. So, if you keep following their commands like blind dogs in the hope of some miserable medals, then they'll rip this world apart into pieces and you are going to be the ammunition in that deed. You are born a human, so act like one, not for god's sake, but for your children's sake.

Fight against the enemies within your state, before you go looking for enemies outside. The biggest enemies of the state are those politicians who look to win a war, instead of organizing the peace, and the citizens who allow them to do so. So, if you want to end a war, don't wait for the orders to come in - stand up and demand from the government to focus on peace and not on war, and if they ignore you, which they most likely would, then forget their intervention and go over to the other side yourself as a vulnerable and unarmed citizen of not a nation, but of peace. And when one side of the border has a handful of such citizens of peace, then the other side is bound to reciprocate that peace. Forget the constitution, forget sovereignty, forget your so-called devotion to your homeland, and for once in your life, devote yourself to the making of peace, because if you don't, then your children will be born in a land so narrow and wild, that they will curse you for giving birth to them in a primitive society.

They will breathe in gun powder instead of oxygen, they will bathe in blood, instead of water and they will live inside the wreckage of buildings instead of a home. Is this the world you have in mind for your beloved progeny? Is this the future you hope to give to the apple of your eye? Think - put down the weapon and think. Turn off the news and think. Silence your phone and think. Open your eyes and think.

For the sake of your children, start thinking now, instead of leaving all the thinking to the government. Because you leave all the thinking to the government, they can make you dance at their fingertips however they want, whenever they want. And when you realize that you are being controlled like some puppets, you yell out loud that your government is corrupt, that you want a new government. And, once you have a new government, then again you let all the decisions of your life made by the new government and naively believe that things would now be different, except it never is different, because the democracy that governments of the world are founded upon, is fundamentally flawed. And when democracy is flawed, the nation it creates, ends up flawed as well. And in the end, such democracy turns nation against nation and people against people.

People are kept unaware of the reality, with the sweet and illusive candy of nationalism. They are made to believe in their bones that killing people in the name of sovereignty is the most glorious act of all - they are made to believe that the citizens of the neighboring country are their arch-enemies - they are made to believe that nationality is far greater than humanity. They are made to believe that surgical strikes against the nation across the border is a great patriotic deed - they are made to believe that raising wall and separating children from their parents are deeds of great glory.

In short, politicians (not all, exceptions include Bernie Sanders, Justin Trudeau and some others) in the government keep doing whatever they desire, and the citizens choose to keep their mouth silent in obedience because that to them is the greatest act of patriotism. In short, to these spineless citizens, their country is always right and the neighboring country is always wrong - their country is always good and the neighboring country is always evil - their country is always on the side of ethics and morality, and the neighboring country is always on the side of moral degradation. And this has been going on since the rise of human civilization across the world. When will this change, one wonders!

And the answer is now. You change - just you - you the individual - you the one human - and slowly but surely, little by little, the entire society will change. Change is contagious, but that contagion has to begin from someone - so, why can't that contagion start from you! Be the contagion of change to the society, only then, can the society evolve into something more humane and less discriminatory and segregational. To create a segregation free society, the individual human must rise breaking all the mental chains of segregation, and I mean all – the chains of nationality, the chains of religion, the chains of language and so on.

The point is, segregation in the society is born from segregation in the mind, so, when the mind is free from segregation, the society is bound to be free from segregation. But remember, it's easier said than done, because harsh and uncivilized though it may sound, segregation is natural, whereas egalitarianism is not.

The segregated and rather limited outlook of our ancestors in the jungle enabled them to stay strong and united in their small tribal communities. But since then, the very notion of community has changed radically - today, in our global society, community means not a tiny little tribe, rather a species called humankind. In such a world, segregating against our own kind, will only bring destruction upon our global community. Every human in every corner of the world is part of our community. No human is foreign to no one - thinking of any human as a foreigner is the most inhuman act of all.

Rise, O Patriots of The Planet!

People's search for power is an illusion, because power itself is an illusion, and till this day, this illusion keeps isolating people from people. People create their own little groups and lock themselves in, and they call that prison sovereignty. They live in their own little wells and have no clue that they can become a part of the great ocean out there - they only hear stories of the ocean - they dream of travelling to that ocean, and sometimes they do, but in their mind they always are stuck in the well, as a result, power hungry bigots can turn them against their own kind in the name of either superiority or sovereignty of their own well over that of others. Let me tell you a story.

Once upon a time, there was a frog that lived in a well. It had lived there for a long time. It was born there and brought up there, and yet was a little, small frog. One day another frog that lived in the sea came and fell into the well.

"Where are you from?" asked the frog of the well.

"I am from the sea."

"The sea! How big is that? Is it as big as my well?" and it took a leap from one side of the well to the other.

"My friend," said the frog of the sea, "how do you compare the sea with your little well?"

Then the frog took another leap and asked, "Is your sea this big?"

"What nonsense you speak, to compare the sea with your well!"

"Well, then," said the frog of the well, "nothing can be bigger than my well; you are a damn liar, get out of here."

This has been the difficulty with the human species since the beginning of civilization. Each human spends the limited few scores of his or her life inside the narrow and rather prejudiced bounds of his or her own well and tries to measure the whole world in comparison with it, be it the well of nation, religion or political affiliation.

As result, only a handful of people amidst the population of seven billion, can truly realize what it's like to live as a liberated human being. Yet, without this fundamental force of liberation, no amount of sovereignty and power can bring real peace and harmony on this planet.

Individuals can be wise, but people are stupid - because, in the fight against the elements of nature, it's the collective stupidity, that is, blind obedience, of our ancestors towards the brave and charismatic chief, that made them survive through the darkest days and fiercest nights. And this blind instinctual urge for following an alpha still prevails in the blueprint of the human psyche, which often drives them quite subconsciously towards obvious self-destruction. Think of the current presidency of our beloved land of liberty for example.

Here, what we must understand is that, if we speak empirically, then there is no such thing as stupid or wise in the kingdom of nature, for the kingdom of nature is governed by only one quality, and that is survival potential. If a behavior exists, it does so, because it has some sort of survival potential attached to it. And this is the reason why scholars, such as scientists and philosophers are way less appealing to the masses in comparison to entertainers such as filmstars, singers or sportspersons.

Scholars (including scientists, philosophers, doctors, teachers, innovators and many more, involved in the practice of science, technology and philosophy) make some of the most significant contributions in the life and growth of the human species - take away the scholars and all progress will come to a standstill, yet most of them spend their life in anonymity outside the tiny circle of their distinct field.

On the other hand, entertainers are seen by people from all walks of life as some sort of all-knowing prophet - if they say, a certain health drink is good, the masses would most naively embrace that health drink in their life - if they say, a certain watch or perfume or handbag is the symbol of elegance, the masses would most blindly run after it - and if they run for office, the masses would most stupidly vote for them, without actually knowing their psychological capacity to run a people and maintain peace.

Here, I beg you not to think of all entertainers to be stupid, rather what I am pointing out is that, the expertise of an entertainer is in entertaining, so you should give them as much reverence as they deserve, not more than that. They are not expert in medical issues - they are not expert in running a people - they are not expert in anything except their work in entertainment - just like, I am not an expert in Chemistry or Physics or Mathematics - I am a Biologist and that's where all my attention is placed. So, if you have a question about Quantum Physics, you must not ask me, rather you must ask a Physicist. And the same is true for every other expert in the world - be it an expert of science, mathematics or arts.

For example, my favorite actors are Cary Grant and Jimmy Stewart, and I enjoy their work immensely, but I don't expect them to have a deep insight into human nature, just because they were and still remain quite famous – that's my job, just like their job was to hold up a mirror in front of the society through their acting, through their work of art.

Now the big question is, why do people fall prey to the charm of celebrities and confuse their charisma to be the sign of wisdom, in most cases quite subconsciously? When our ancestors lived in the jungle amidst other animals, the chances of survival of the tribe increased in proportion to their blind loyalty to the alpha, a public figure with leadership characteristics, which mostly consisted of an absurd amount of confidence and charm. And this evolutionary instinct of attraction to confidence and charm still remains rather dominant in the common human psyche, which makes them vulnerable to the spell of charisma, even if that charisma has no content of character or wisdom underneath it.

In everyday life of the common human, reason takes a back seat and emotions dictate all significant behavior. "Erase the emotions and you would erase the most important part of what it's like to be human" (as I said in Mission Reality). In short, no matter what you say, if you can say it with such a confidence that it touches people at an emotional level, then you can make them believe in anything - you can make them think anything - you can make them do anything.

People do not care about right or wrong - they don't care about truth and reasoning - they are subconsciously driven by their instinct for survival, towards confidence, charm and charisma, just like moths are drawn towards a burning candle to face their inevitable demise.

The point is, you can take the human out of the jungle, but you can't take the jungle out of the human, not so fast anyways - it'll take time, a very very long time, to successfully incapacitate our tribal and savage instincts, but that too will happen only and only if you the individual stand up to your own primitive elements and act as human - free, civilized and conscientious.

And the individuals who have the most potential to stand up to their innate primitiveness, are the youth - the young lions, whose blood is boiling with vigour, and all they need is the right push. Youth - o my brave, mad and naïve youth - what are you waiting for - forget tradition - forget possibility and impossibility - forget name, fame and security - forget the ill-gotten games of survival - and work - give your everything to your society - the old and the frail cannot, but you can - and you must - because if you don't, then who else! Do you feel the immediacy my friend - do you feel the urgency - do you feel it in your bones, like you feel hot in the summer and chills in the winter - do you?

So, what are you waiting for - are you waiting for somebody to magically appear in your life and show you the way - because if you are, then you'll spend the rest of your life waiting and hoping - and nothing will ever change, neither for you, nor for your society. So, stop waiting and stand up - stand up with vigor, speak up with confidence and act with conscience.

Take the responsibility of your whole society on your shoulders and act. Destroy yourself if needed, but never let bigotry, injustice and misfortune destroy the lives of others. Many will dislike you - many will despise you - and even more will pity you as lost souls, but pay no heed to them, pay attention to your work only.

Remember, in a thousand years, nobody will remember the naysayers and meek worshippers, but your work will write your name upon the very fabric of time in golden engravings. Mark you, there is no greater power than the power of youth. Give me ten conscientious youth from each nation, and I'll change the course of human progress.

Some may say, what's the urgency! I am afraid, those who think and say so, are the ones who never in their life contribute a single substantial deed in the path of progress, not willingly anyways - so, to them I say, if you can't contribute, don't mock those who do or undermine their confidence by questioning their sense of urgency. Urgency is the need of this hour and if you don't feel it, then it only means, your purpose on this earth, is only to populate it, not unlike all other animals on earth.

And remember, age is a question of mind over matter - if you don't mind, it doesn't matter. So, everything I mentioned addressing the youth, applies to anybody who feels young and energetic at heart. Anybody who has a death-defying zeal to bring a change, is capable of bringing that change. All that matters, is action, nothing short of that would do.

Anybody can populate a planet, by consent or by force, but to master the forces of a planet, it takes valour, curiosity and a ton of insanity - insanity for justice, insanity for equality, insanity for upliftment - without this insanity in a handful of lionhearts, no amount of sanity can lift up the torch of progress. Be vigorous, be insane and use your force of life for the good of your people, your society, your humankind, nay, our humankind. Remember, our kind is our responsibility, and to lift them up, if we have to walk on the agonizingly sharp edge of a sword all through our life, then be it. To hell with our future - if by sacrificing our present, we can create a bright and humane future for our humankind, then such sacrifice is the most delightful fulfillment of our lifeforce.

Life is a force and when that force is used to breathe life in the existence of others, then there is no greater fulfillment of that force than that. A glass of water has no value on its own, but the moment it quenches the thirst of an exhausted person, it turns more valuable than gold. Be a glass of water and quench the thirst of others. A glass of water doesn't need any fancy introduction to be hailed important, it doesn't need pomp and ceremony to be seen as significant, it doesn't need any fancy attire to appear appealing, all it needs to do is be there for the thirsty.

So, just be there for the people in need - for the people in misery - for the people struck by misfortune. Pour down on people like showers of monsoon and breathe life into their droughtful existence. Flow in their life like a whiff of fresh air and take away all their exhaustions. Sail through their veins like an unsinkable vessel and stir up vigor in their blood torrents. Act in their life as an indomitable force for good, and in time, all will be good for humanity.

Do something so grand with your life that you can speak out loud to the naysayers, not with arrogance, but with self-respect - "if you die, you'll be forgotten in a week, like any other animal on earth, but when I die, my name will be an inspiration to thousands of generations to come."

I live not to breed humans, I live to breed Gods. The world has enough humans to keep reproducing, but a few lions - a few Gods - a few Lords of Time, must give up all that reproduction business and sacrifice all their lifeforce at the altar of service and progress. Because without the sacrifice of these Gods, future generations will not have a civilized and progressive society to live with dignity and freedom. Here I am not advocating for absolute celibacy, but what I'm pointing out is, the priority of the Gods must always be first the benefit of the society, then everything else.

Adopt the society and raise it like your own child. There is no greater church than the society and serving the society means serving Almighty, because Almighty exists nowhere else, but in each human being. Helping a human means worshipping the Lord. And there is no greater and holier worship than that - it's the worship without pomp and ceremony, yet it's the worship most divine. Helping a human is equivalent of a hundred pilgrimages. No pilgrimage is holier than compassion, no gospel is truer than kindness, no offering is grander than love.

Offer yourself at the feet of others, and your very existence will turn into a torch of holiness. And as I have already explained countless times in my previous works, humanness is holiness. So, being human is being holy. The real holy grail is the human mind itself. If you are a human in your mind, then you have all the holiness in the world, but if your actions scream prejudice, discrimination and bigotry, then no matter how human you look, you still are an animal.

They say spirituality distinguishes a human from the animals, but I say, spirituality filled with mystical nonsense is nothing but a sign of animal behavior, whereas, spirituality that manifests in a person through acts of kindness and acceptance, is what truly distinguishes a human from the animal. Remember, we all are born animals, it's only with our acts of humanity can we become truly human. And that becoming human is the truest salvation of all. Salvation is no possession of supernaturalism, rather it's the most fundamental ingredient of human existence, without which, human life is not human life, but animal life.

Organically speaking, there is no difference between human life and animal life, for we humans are animals as well. But when we delve deeper into the psychological significance of the term "human", we begin to discover the fathomless grandeur of the term. You know what it means to be human? It means justice coming out of your synapses - it means equality bursting out of your arteries - it means your footsteps causing an avalanche of acceptance.

Every step you take, must herald the advent of a more humane and less discriminatory society. And with those self-aware and humane footsteps, will we witness the manifestation of a truly civilized and united world, where there will be only one sovereignty, that is, sovereignty of the humankind. In that sovereign world, external borders may or may not exist, but in the mind of each human, there will be no place for any border that could essentially separate a human from another human.

Who is I, who is the other, it's all I. The other is I, and I is the other, it's all one. One is not one, but a reflection of all, and all is not all, but a reflection of one. So, what one does, can make an impact on all, and what all do, can make an impact on the one. One must be responsible for all, and all must be responsible for the one. Because without responsibility, no one is civilized, no all is civilized and as such, no one can have a humane world and no all can have a humane world.

We no longer have the primitive luxury to take pride in the wars between nations, cold or otherwise. In any war, except that for freedom from oppression, victory of any nation, is the defeat of all nations, because each war comes at the cost of lives, in the name of the same old tribal loyalty. And it's high time that we free this world of ours from the binds of primitive tribalism masquerading as pompous ideologies.

Blinded by the glaring shine of progress, people think all the need for revolution is over, now that you have a safe and secure world. Think again. Your tiny little neighborhood may have all the comfort of modern life, but there are still countless lands across the world, that lack the very basic amenities of life - in these places, justice, peace, sleep, food, water, shelter, are still stories from the Arabian Nights. So, how can you, a creature of conscience and character sleep so sound, on your soft and cozy bed? How my friend?

Throw away the sheets, get down from your pedestal of luxury and run to those lands of misery as the rising sun and give your all to instill the basic rights in their helpless existence, so that at least the unborn could be born in an environment that's more humane than savage, that's more just than immoral, that's more accepting than discriminatory, and that's more evolving than stagnant.

The need for a revolution has arisen again, except this time, it's not for freedom from obvious oppression of external forces, rather, this time the revolution is far too consequential, it's the revolution for freedom from our internal forces of primitiveness, the primitiveness that makes us hate neighbors from the other side of the border, the primitiveness that makes us hate love that's not between opposites, the primitiveness that makes us hate belief that's not akin to our own, the primitiveness that makes us favor people based on not their character but their status and charisma.

It's high time that we grab hold of our own primitiveness instead of letting them get hold of our character. It's time that our character exudes a bright, gentle light that once caste upon the world, does not discriminate between the poor and the rich, between the white and the black, between the learned and the illiterate, between the native and the foreigner. Light knows no bigotry, wind knows no discrimination, rain knows no snobbery, crops know no segregation.

Remember, it's not enough to have independence. You must know how to utilize that independence responsibly. Independence means responsibility, not recklessness. Independence without responsibility is barbarism. If we don't take responsibility of what happens to our society, then no amount of independence can improve human condition.

Think of the world of the jungle - it is the most independent way of life you can think of, for there is no rule in the jungle except the rule of survival. But such independence is not something that goes well in a civilized society such as ours, for such extreme independence is only savagery, yet such is the independence, most of the human population still craves for, and that's the reason why a functional society of humans, though called civilized, still needs the apparatus called "law" to keep humans from practicing the extreme independence of the wild. So, it's not independence that we should be aiming at, rather our aim should be to raise the sense of responsibility, first in ourselves, then in our children.

Be a responsible human and instill the same sense of responsibility within the children, by being an example in front of them. Don't just teach them to be protective of their independence and sovereignty, rather raise citizens of peace, whose blood would be teeming with responsibility and conscience.

Weakness is degrading, so is courage without responsibility. To unite this whole world with the thread of acceptance and harmony, may sound like a titanic task, but all it takes is one generation of conscientious and responsible citizens in each nation - if only these handful of young members of the society around the world take up the responsibility to raise, not citizens of a nation, but citizens of a planet, then no force in the world can keep the process of human unification from manifesting in front of our very eyes.

Give them the courage to speak, but more than that, instill in them the capacity to be aware of the implications of what they speak. Freedom of speech is a fallacy, it is not absolute. It can be hailed absolute only if the person possessing it, has the conscience to distinguish the right from the wrong, justice from injustice, acceptance from discrimination. Having the freedom of speech doesn't mean saying whatever you want, it means saying what's humane, hateless and non-prejudicial. So, raise not only courage and dignity in the children, but awareness as well - awareness of the implications of their words, of their actions, of their behavior in the society.

Behavior - that's the key, not just good behavior or decent behavior, rather genuine responsible behavior. And genuine responsible behavior rises from genuine non-prejudicial thoughts. And genuine non-prejudicial thoughts rise from a genuine will for understanding. Do you want to understand? Is that will of yours strong enough to trample all egotism and socio-cultural conditioning? If yes, then there is hope for responsibility in your behavior, and from that individual behavior, rises responsibility in your society. Remember, there is no distinction between personal and social. What's personal, is social - what's social, is personal.

All issues in the society prevail, because the person thinks, the self is separate from the society. And this is the gravest mistake that any sentient species could ever make. With great sentience, comes great responsibility. Unless you the individual realize this in your bones, nothing will ever change in the society you live. For the society to change, the self must utilize the fullest potential of its sentience. Sentience is a huge deal - it cannot be taken for granted, because by doing so, we will only be belittling our own capacities. And it is as capital a mistake to belittle oneself, as it is to boast about oneself.

Know your capacities, know your shortcomings, and bring out all your powers to improve human condition in your society. And you don't need to start big, start small - start with improving human condition in your neighborhood, and your work will inspire a few more to do the same. And eventually human condition around the world will be improved.

Work for the corner of the world that you are in, not because only that corner is your own corner and other corners are foreign, but because we must start the change from where we stand. It's not the place that counts, it's the action. Improving the living condition of even one person, is equivalent of improving the living condition of an entire species. It all begins with one person - one entity - one organism. Think of the very kingdom of life on earth for example. This vast domain of lifeforms came to existence from a single cell.

So, if a single cell can populate an entire planet, then an individual can change an entire society. So, the question is, not, can one person change the world, rather it is, is the person driven enough - like the religious terrorists for example! The so-called "religious" terrorists are ridiculously driven to spread the supremacy of their own religion over all others, and to achieve that they are even willing to sacrifice their life. If only we could see such drive, such immense passion for an idea, in the humans of conscience and character, then we could erase all injustice, all discrimination, all segregation, in mere decades.

But alas, people are busy sleeping - they are busy snoring in their bed, after a hearty dinner and some good, wholesome sex. Then they wake up and run to the office, and after work, they come back home and then start over the cycle the next day. This goes on, until the call of death arrives. So, now the question is, when are they going to do something substantial for the society they live in! And they may say, the problems of the society, are not their business, they are the government's business.

And that's where all the trouble of our world begins - in relying for every little thing on the so-called government. Naturally, the governments all over the world have become accustomed to do with the citizens and with the nations, as they desire. And if this goes on, then no amount of pretend peace talks in some pretend united nations, is going to bring real peace on this planet.

To bring real peace, the individual, regardless of their walk of life, must break their cycle of rat race and make time to work for their society, as much as they work for their family. The society is our family, that's the only way we could ever construct a world of united humans. It's difficult, very difficult, but not impossible, and not fictitious either. It is very much possible, but to make it, the very term difficulty must vanish from your psyche, and what must rise, is the genuine sense of responsibility.

Nothing is higher than the humans, not the government, not the politics, not the nation, and not even the constitution, for all of these, are human constructs, and no human construct is flawless. So, in order to not fall prey to the flaws of the government, of the politics, of the nation, of the constitution, we must place the interest of the people first and then everything else.

One may say, aren't the government, the politics, the nation and the constitution about the interest of the people? And the answer is, in theory it is indeed supposed to be so, but in practice, the whole scenario is absolutely opposite. There is always a great difference between a theory and its practical implications. For example, feminism is in theory about equal rights of all humans regardless of gender, but in practice, it has become the feminine counterpart of patriarchal oppression and aggression. Likewise, humanism is in theory about equal rights of humans regardless of faith, but in practice, it has become the atheist counterpart of religious extremism. So, just because the term indicates something just and impartial, doesn't mean it actually is when put to practice in the society of the creatures known as humans.

Humans are lamentably insecure creatures, that's why they build various psychological patterns to feel secure inside them. And in the process, they separate themselves from each other, simply due to the illusive barriers of each other's patterns. And when they do not want people from other patterns to disrespect their own pattern, they construct another illusive psychological apparatus called "free speech" or "freedom to express one's opinion". And then when this illusive mental construct makes them confront with actual discrimination, they get baffled and try to figure out a solution through another illusive apparatus of the human society called the "law".

And advocates of law condition the rest of the population to believe that law and justice are one and the same thing, whereas they are completely contradictory. In fact, the presence of law implies the presence of injustice, not justice. Justice is not the exclusive possession of some politicians and bureaucrats, whereas law is.

Today, people in administration manipulate law to serve their own interest and then they present a doctored version of justice to the public based on their manipulated, self-serving version of law. So, to the law enforcement officials I say, "uphold not law, but justice, for when you uphold law, you need to explain yourself to your superiors, but when you uphold justice, you do not need to explain your actions to anyone, for your very actions will be the testament of justice".

Law dictates discriminatory opinions are not illegal as long as the discriminated does not press defamation charges. Which means, discrimination is not discrimination, if it's not reported to the law - and this also means, injustice is not injustice, if it's not reported to the law.

People love to say, everybody is entitled to their opinions. It is one of the greatest fallacies of human habit. Everybody is not entitled to their opinion, not when their opinion advocates for segregation and discrimination. As I said earlier, freedom of speech doesn't mean saying whatever one wants, it means saying what's non-discriminatory, non-prejudicial and non-barbarian. Bigots may have the right to say that all Mexicans are drug smugglers, all black and brown people are inferior humans, or all non-muslims are infidels, inside the narrow bounds of their own house, but they are not entitled to express such opinion, when amidst people, amidst a civilized society.

Remember, acceptance of bigotry and discrimination is the same as advocating for bigotry and discrimination. To be a part of a civilized society, the human must, not should, but must foster their opinion on humane and non-discriminatory grounds. If not - if they begin to advocate for prejudice, segregation and discrimination instead, then it becomes the responsibility of the civilized and conscientious humans around to stand up to those human-looking apes, not with aggression, but with gentle but bold humanitarian voice.

Do you have that voice, my friend? Do you? Because if you do, then the world could use that, since it's lacking in humane voices. There are too many people to speak up for their religion, for their country, for their language and so on, but very few to speak for the humankind. So speak up, for every word that you utter, every action that you take, with humanitarian responsibility, will contribute a great deal in eradicating parts of the discrimination that has polluted our beautiful planet. And if you choose not to speak up and stay deaf, dumb and blind instead, then take this oath - "all bigots, fundamentalists and sectarianists are my bosom friends - I shall always be faithful to them - I shall always stand by them, no matter how inhuman they behave - and I shall always do my best to promote their atrocities by maintaining my silence in the face of prejudice, hatred and inhumanism".

In short, if a person says, white people are a superior race to others, or all non-believers are destined to burn in hell, or all homosexuals are sinners, then such a person is not entitled to his opinions, because his opinions do not belong in a civilized and conscientious society. Of course, nobody is stopping him to go into the jungle and shout as much as he wants, his savage opinions amidst the wild animals, since he himself is one.

The point is, just because somebody has a strong belief about something, doesn't mean that belief belongs in a civilized society. In most cases, nay, in all cases, beliefs are not created based on reality, reality is created based on beliefs. Which means, if we turn a deaf ear to those barbarian beliefs and opinions advocating most loudly for their exclusive supremacy above all reason, then they will only create a barbarian and discriminatory societal reality. And no conscientious individual with a beating heart inside the skull can allow it to happen!

Therefore, all beliefs and opinions must be scrutinized with the force of reason and compassion. Remember, not all beliefs have to make sense, but all beliefs at the very least, must be free from segregation, only then can they be entitled to expression in the society. Let me elaborate, I have friends, from all walks of life from around the world, some of them are believers, some non-believers, some non-dualists, and so on. Their belief or disbelief in a supernatural higher force or entity doesn't bother me the least, as long as they do not look down on people holding different belief systems. In a civilized, humane and inclusive world, a person's behavior with others is most important, not belief.

It's an inclusive and humane world that we must work to build, since we have already wasted a great deal of time in building and maintaining a tribalistic world. And now is the time to discard the tribalism and dive into humanism - not the anti-religious kind of humanism, but plain ordinary humanism, where the humans come first, then everything else.

Humanism means not hating religions, it means not hating beliefs, it means not hating faith, but what it means is to stand by the humans, speak for the humans and empower the humans, crossing race, religion and creed. Humanism is not anti-anything, except anti-segregation - humanism is not against anything, except against prejudices and hate - humanism is not afraid of anything, except of losing touch with basic human needs, not just of the body, but of the mind. So, be afraid, be extreme and be absurd - be afraid of losing touch - be extreme in accepting others - and be absurd in serving society.

And remember, it's very much likely that no one will care for your agonies and miseries, if you choose the path of service over the path of everyday pleasures. To them you will be a pillar of strength, standing high and quite lifeless to erase people's miseries and confusions. For example, I am like the Vatican or Mecca, people love visiting there once in a while to find solution to their problems and confusions, but no one likes living there. Such is and will always be the predicament of the path of servitude and sacrifice. Knowing this, if you still can't hold yourself from running to the aid of the helpless and downtrodden, then my friend, there is no power in any obscurity to keep you from uplifting the society.

Society, society and society, this should be on your mind 24/7. Only then will there be hope for some change, some progress, some improvement in your corner of the world. We are not an advanced species – not when millions of our sisters and brothers still go hungry - not when countless of our siblings still don't have a roof over their head - not when many still spend every second of their life in fear of being bombed to death. And to change this, we need sacrifice - sacrifice of bravehearts - sacrifice of young lions and bold tigresses - sacrifice of boiling blood.

Remember, what the youth can achieve in ten years, will take the elderly a thousand years. So, awake my boiling bravehearts - arise my passionate patriots - and give to the world - give to the world your sleep - give to the world your serenity - give to the world your security - and above all, give to the world your youth.

Mark you, there is nothing more powerful, more impactful and more far-reaching than the wit and will of young humans - so dedicate all your wit and all your will, in the betterment of the world you are born in, so that the opportunities and the virtues that our society lacks today, will be available plenty when we hand over this beautiful world of ours to the humans yet to born. It's not a promise, for promises can be broken - it's a responsibility, which must be carried out, so long as we see ourselves as humans. And this very responsibility towards the society is the greatest and highest religion of the citizens of peace.

BIBLIOGRAPHY

Archer M., (2000), Being Human: The Problem of Agency. Cambridge University Press.

Archer M., (2003), Structure, Agency and the Internal Conversation. Cambridge University Press.

Adolphs R (2003) Cognitive neuroscience of human social behaviour. Nature Rev Neurosci 4: 165–178.

Adolphs R, Tranel D, Damasio AR (2003) Dissociable neural systems for recognizing emotions. Brain Cogn 52: 61–69.

Afton, A. D. (1985). Forced copulation as a reproductive strategy of male lesser scaup: A field test of some predictions. - Behaviour 92, p. 146-167.

Allison T, Puce A, McCarthy G. (2000) Social perception from visual cues: role of the STS region. Trends Cogn Sci 4: 267–278.

Andresen, Jensine, and Robert Forman, eds. Cognitive Models and Spiritual Maps. Bowling Green, Ohio: Imprint Academic, 2000.

Ashbrook, James, and Carol Albright. The Humanizing Brain: Where Religion and Neuroscience Meet. Cleveland, OH: Pilgrim Press, 1997.

Azari, Nina, Janpeter Nickel, Gilbert Wunderlich, Michael Niedeggen, Harald Hefter, Lutz Tellmann, Hans Herzog, Petra Stoerig, Dieter Birnbacher, and Rudiger Seitz. "Neural Correlates of Religious Experience." European Journal of Neuroscience 13, no. 8 (2001)

Agar, N. (2004). Liberal eugenics: In defence of human enhancement. London: Blackwell Publishing.

Alteheld, N., Roessler, G., Vobig, M., & Walter, R. (2004). The retina implant new approach to a visual prosthesis. Biomedizinische Technik, 49(4), 99–103.

Antal, A., Nitsche, M. A., Kincses, T. Z., Kruse, W., Hoffmann, K. P., & Paulus, W. (2004a). Facilitation of visuo-motor learning by transcranial direct current stimulation of the motor and extrastriate visual areas in humans. European Journal of Neuroscience, 19(10), 2888–2892.

Bhat Z, Kumar, S, Bhat H (2015) In vitro meat production. Challenges and benefits over conventional meat production. J Sci Food Agric 14: 241–248

Bernstein R. J., (1967), John Dewey. New York: Washington Square Press.

Bernstein R.J., (1971), Praxis and Action: Contemporary Philosophies of Human Activity. Philadelphia: University of Pennsylvania Press.

Bernstein R.J., (1976), The Restructuring Social and Political Thought.

Bernstein R.J., (1983), Beyond Relativism and Objectivism: Science, Hermeneutics, and Praxis. Philadelphia: University of Pennsylvania Press.

Bernstein R.J., (1986), Philosophical Profiles. Philadelphia: University of Pennsylvania Press.

Bernstein R.J., (1991), New Constellation. Cambridge: MIT Press.

Barash, D. P. (1977). Sociobiology of rape in mallards (Anas platyrhynchos): Responses of the mated male. - Science 197, p. 788-789.

Berger, J. (1986). Wild horses of the great basin: Social competition and population size. - The University of Chicago Press, Chicago.

Birkhead, T. R., Johnson, S. D. & Nettleship, D. N. (1985). Extra-pair matings and mate guarding in the common murre Uria aalge. - Anim. Behav. 33, p. 608-619.

Beauregard, Mario, and Vincent Paquette. "Neural Correlates of a Mystical Experience in Carmelite Nuns." Neuroscience Letters 405, no. 3 (2006)

Benson, Herbert. Timeless Healing: The Power and Biology of Belief. New York: Scribner, 1996

Bogen, J.E.(1995a), 'On the neurophysiology of consciousness: Part I. An overview', Consciousness and Cognition, 4.

Bogen, J.E. (1995b), 'On the neurophysiology of consciousness: Part II. Constraining the semantic problem', Consciousness and Cognition, 4.

Bremner, J. D., R. Soufer, et al. (2001). "Gender differences in cognitive and neural correlates of remembrance of emotional words." Psychopharmacol Bull 35 (3).

Brothers, L. (2002). The social brain: A project for integrating primate behavior and neurophysiology in a new domain. In J. T. Cacioppo et al. (Eds.), Foundations in neuroscience. Cambridge, MA: MIT Press.

Buss, D. D. (2003). Evolutionary Psychology: The New Science of Mind, 2nd ed. New York: Allyn & Bacon.

Buss, D. M. (1989). "Conflict between the sexes: Strategic interference and the evocation of anger and upset." J Pers Soc Psychol 56 (5).

Buss, D. M. (1995). "Psychological sex differences. Origins through sexual selection." Am Psychol 50 (3).

Buss, D. M. (2002). "Review: Human Mate Guarding." Neuro Endocrinol Lett 23 (Suppl 4).

Buss, D. M., and D. P. Schmitt (1993). "Sexual strategies theory: An evolutionary perspective on human mating." Psychol Rev 100 (2).

Blakemore SJ, Decety J (2001) From the perception of action to the understanding of intention. Nature Rev Neurosci 2: 561.

Bruce C, Desimone R, Gross CG (1981) Visual properties of neurons in a polysensory area in superior temporal sulcus of the macaque. J Neurophysiol 46: 369–384.

Buccino G, Vogt S, Ritzl A, Fink GR, Zilles K, Freund HJ, Rizzolatti G (2004) Neural circuits underlying imitation of hand actions: an event related fMRI study. Neuron 42: 323–34.

Colapietro V., (1988), "Human Agency: The Habits of Our Being."

Southern Journal of Philosophy, XXVI, 2, pp. 153-68.

Colapietro V., (1992), "Purpose, Power, and Agency." The Monist, 75, 4 (October) pp. 423-44.

Colapietro V., (2003), "Signs and their vicissitudes: Meanings in excess of consciousness and functionality." Logica, Dialogica, Ideologica, a cure di Susan Petrilli e Patrizia Calefato (Milano: Mimesis), pp. 221-36.

Colapietro V., (2004a), "C. S. Peirce's Reclamation of Teleology." Nature in American Philosophy, ed. Jean De Groot (Washington, D.C.: Catholic University Press of America), pp. 88-108.

Colapietro V., (2004b), "Portrait of a Historicist: An Alternative Reading of Peircean Semiotic." Semiotiche, 2/04 [maggio 2004], pp. 49-68.

Colapietro V., (2006), "Engaged Pluralism: Between Alterity and

Sociality." The Pragmatic Century: Conversations with Richard J. Bernstein (Albany, NY: SUNY Press), pp. 39-68.

Colapietro V., (2009), "Habit, Competence, and Purpose." Forthcoming in The Transactions of the Charles S. Peirce Society.

Calder AJ, Keane J, Manes F, Antoun N, Young AW (2000) Impaired recognition and experience of disgust following brain injury. Nature Neurosci 3: 1077–1078.

Carey DP, Perrett DI, Oram MW (1997) Recognizing, understanding and reproducing actions. In: Jeannerod M, Grafman J (eds) Handbook of neuropsychology. Vol. 11: Action and cognition. Elsevier, Amsterdam.

Carr L, Iacoboni M, Dubeau MC, Mazziotta JC, Lenzi GL (2003) Neural mechanisms of empathy in humans: a relay from neural systems for imitation to limbic areas. Proc Natl Acad Sci USA 100: 5497–5502.

Changeux JP, Ricoeur P (1998) La nature et la règle. Odile Jacob, Paris.

Cochin S, Barthelemy C, Roux S, Martineau J (1999) Observation and execution of movement: similarities demonstrated by quantified electroencephalograpy. Eur J Neurosci 11: 1839– 1842.

Chomsky Noam, (2017) Requiem for the American Dream

Chomsky Noam, (2016) Who Rules the World?

Chomsky Noam, (2010) How the World Works

Churchland, P.S. (1986), Neurophilosophy (Cambridge, MA: The MIT Press).

Churchland, P.S. & Ramachandran, V.S. (1993), 'Filling in: Why Dennett is wrong', in Dennett and His Critics: Demystifying Mind, ed. B. Dahlbom (Oxford: Blackwell Scientific Press).

Churchland, P.S., Ramachandran, V.S. & Sejnowski, T.J. (1994), 'A critique of pure vision', in Large- scale Neuronal Theories of the Brain, ed. C. Koch & J.L. Davis (Cambridge, MA: The MIT Press).

Crick, F. (1994), The Astonishing Hypothesis: The Scientific Search for the Soul (New York: Simon and Schuster).

Crick, F. (1996), 'Visual perception: rivalry and consciousness', Nature, 379.

Crick, F. & Koch, C. (1992), 'The problem of consciousness', Scientific American, 267.

Craig AD (2002) How do you feel? Interoception: the sense of the physiological condition of the body. Nature Rev Neurosci 3: 655–666.

Damasio, A (2003a) Looking for Spinoza. Harcourt Inc. Damasio A (2003b) Feeling of emotion and the self. Ann NY Acad Sci 1001: 253–261.

d'Aquili, Eugene. "Senses of Reality in Science and Religion." Zygon 17, no 4 (1982)

d'Aquili, Eugene. "The Biopsychological Determinants of Religious Ritual Behavior." Zygon 10, no. 1 (1975)

d'Aquili, Eugene. "The Myth-Ritual Complex: A Biogenetic Structural Analysis." Zygon 18, no. 3 (1983)

d'Aquili, Eugene, and Andrew Newberg. The Mystical Mind: Probing the Biology of Religious Experience. Minneapolis: Fortress Press, 1999.

Daly DD. 1958. Ictal affect. Am J Psychiatry.

Damasio, A. (1994) Descartes' Error: Emotion, Reason and the Human Brain. New York, Putnams.

Damasio, A. (1999) The Feeling of What Happens: Body, Emotion and the Making of Consciousness. London, Heinemann.

Darwin, C. (1859) On the Origin of Species by Means of Natural Selection. London, Murray.

Darwin, C. (1871) The Descent of Man and Selection in Relation to Sex. London, John Murray.

Darwin, C. (1872) The Expression of the Emotions in Man and Animals. London, John Murray; also published 1965, Chicago, University of Chicago Press.

Dawkins, M.S. (1987) Minding and mattering. In C. Blakemore and S. Greenfield (eds) Mindwaves. Oxford, Blackwell, 151-60.

Dawkins, R. (1976) The Selfish Gene. Oxford, Oxford University Press; a new edition, with additional material, was published in 1989.

Dawkins, R. (1986) The Blind Watchmaker. London, Longman.

Di Pellegrino G, Fadiga L, Fogassi L, Gallese V, Rizzolatti G (1992) Understanding motor events: A neurophysiological study. Exp Brain Res 91: 176–80.

Deikman, A.J. (2000) A functional approach to mysticism. Journal of Consciousness Studies 7(11-12), 75-91.

Delmonte, M.M. (1987) Personality and meditation. In M. West (ed.) The Psychology of Meditation. Oxford, Clarendon Press, 118-32.

Dennett, D.C. (1987) The Intentional Stance. Cambridge, MA, MIT Press.

Dennett, D.C. (1988) Quining qualia. In A.J. Marcel and E. Bisiach (eds)

Consciousness in Contemporary Science. Oxford, Oxford University Press, 42-77.

Dennett, D.C. (1991) Consciousness Explained. Boston, MA, and London, Little, Brown and Co.

Dennett, D.C. (1995a) Darwin's Dangerous Idea. London, Penguin.

Dennett, D.C. (1995b) The unimagined preposterousness of zombies. Journal of Consciousness Studies 2(4), 322-6.

Dennett, D.C. (1995c) Cog: steps towards consciousness in robots. In T. Metzinger (ed.) Conscious Experience. Thorverton, Devon, Imprint Academic, 471-87.

Dennett, D.C. (1995d) The path not taken. Behavioral and Brain Sciences 18, 252-3; commentary on N. Block, On a confusion about a function of consciousness. Behavioral and Brain Sciences 18, 227.

Dennett, D.C. (1996a) Facing backwards on the problem of consciousness. Journal of Consciousness Studies 3(1), 4-6.

Dennett, D.C. (1996b) Kinds of Minds: Towards an Understanding of Consciousness. London, Weidenfeld & Nicolson.

Dennett, D.C. (1997) An exchange with Daniel Dennett. In J. Searle (ed.) The Mystery of Consciousness. New York, New York Review of Books, 115-19.

Dennett, D.C. (1998) The myth of double transduction. In S.R. Hameroff, A.W. Kaszniak and A. C. Scott (eds) Toward a Science of Consciousness: The Second Tucson Discussions and Debates. Cambridge, MA, MIT Press, 97-107.

Dennett, D.C. (1998b) Brainchildren: Essays on Designing Minds. Cambridge, MA, MIT Press.

Dennett, D.C. (2001) The fantasy of first person science. Debate with D. Chalmers, Northwestern University, Evanston, IL, February 2001.

Dennett, D.C. (2003) Freedom Evolves. New York, Penguin.

Dennett, D.C. and Kinsbourne, M. (1992) Time and the observer: the where and when of consciousness in the brain. Behavioral and Brain Sciences 15, 183-247, including commentaries and authors' responses.

Dewey J., (1911 [1977]), "Epistemological Realism: The Alleged Ubiquity of the Knowledge Relation." Journal of Philosophy, VIII, 20 (September 28, 1911).

Dewhurst, Kenneth, and A. W. Beard. "Sudden Religious Conversions in Temporal Lobe Epilepsy." British Journal of Psychiatry 117 (1970)

Dewhurst K, Beard AW. Sudden religious conversions in temporal lobe epilepsy. 1970 Epilepsy Behav 2003

Devinsky O, Lai G. Spirituality and religion in epilepsy. Epilepsy Behav 2008.

Devinsky, O., Morrell, MJ, Vogt, BA. (1995) 'Contribution of anterior cingulate cortex to behavior', Brain, 118.

E. Horvitz, "One Hundred Year Study on Artificial Intelligence: Reflections and Framing," ed: Stanford University, 2014.

Eckhart Meister, Selected Writings

Egidi R., ed. (1999), "Von Wright and 'Dante's Dream': Stages in a Philosophical Pilgrim's Progress", in In Search of a New Humanism: the Philosophy of G.H. von Wright, ed. by R. Egidi, Kluwer, Dordrecht.

Fadiga L, Fogassi L, Pavesi G, Rizzolatti G (1995) Motor facilitation during action observation: a magnetic stimulation study. J Neurophysiol 73: 2608–2611.

Fogassi L, Gallese V, Fadiga L, Rizzolatti G (1998) Neurons responding to the sight of goal directed hand/arm actions in the parietal area PF (7b) of the macaque monkey. Soc Neurosci Abs 24:257.5.

Frith U, Frith CD (2003) Development and neurophysiology of mentalizing. Philos Trans R Soc Lond B Biol Sci 358: 459.

Farah, M.J. (1989), 'The neural basis of mental imagery', Trends in Neurosciences, 10.

Finlay BL, Darlington RB (1995) Linked regularities in the development and evolution of mammalian brains. Science 268.

Freud, S. "The Interpretation of Dreams", 1900

Freud, S. "Selected papers on hysteria and other psychoneuroses" Journal of Nervous and Mental Disease 1909.

Freud, S. "The Origin and Development of Psychoanalysis", 1910

Freud, S. "Psychopathology of everyday life", 1914

Freud, S. "Beyond the Pleasure Principle", 1920

Frith, C.D. & Dolan, R.J. (1997), 'Abnormal beliefs: Delusions and memory', Paper presented at the May, 1997, Harvard Conference on Memory and Belief.

Gay, Volney, ed. Neuroscience and Religion. Plymouth, UK: Lexington Books, 2009.

Gazzaniga, M. S. (1985). The social brain. New York: Basic Books.

Gazzaniga, M.S. (1993), 'Brain mechanisms and conscious experience', Ciba Foundation Symposium, 174.

Geschwind N. "Behavioural changes in temporal lobe epilepsy". Psychol Med. 1979.

Gellhorn, E., Kiely, W.F. "Mystical states of consciousness: neurophysiological and clinical aspects." J Nerv Ment Dis. 1972;154:399-405.

Gilbert SL, Dobyns WB, Lahn BT (2005) Genetic links between brain development and brain evolution. Nat Rev Genet 6.

Gray JA. The Psychology of Fear and Stress. 2nd ed. New York, NY: Cambridge University Press; 1988.

Gloor, P. (1992), 'Amygdala and temporal lobe epilepsy', in The Amygdala: Neurobiological Aspects of Emotion, Memory and Mental

Dysfunction, ed J.P. Aggleton (New York: Wiley-Liss).

Greenspan, S. I. and S. G. Shanker (2004). The first idea: How symbols, language, and intelligence evolved from our early primate ancestors to modern humans. Cambridge, MA: Da Capo Press.

Grady, D. (1993), 'The vision thing: Mainly in the brain', Discover, June.

Gallagher HL, Frith CD (2003) Functional imaging of 'theory of mind'. Trends Cogn Sci 7: 77.

Gallese V, Fogassi L, Fadiga L, Rizzolatti G (2002) Action representation and the inferior parietal lobule. In: Prinz W, Hommel B (eds) Attention & Performance XIX. Common mechanisms in perception and action. Oxford University Press, Oxford.

Gallese V, Keysers C, Rizzolatti G (2004) A unifying view of the basis of social cognition. Trends Cogn Sci 8: 396–403.

Gangitano M, Mottaghy FM, Pascual-Leone A (2001) Phase specific modulation of cortical motor output during movement observation. NeuroReport 12: 1489–1492.

Gangitano M, Mottaghy FM, Pascual-Leone A (2004) Modulation of premotor mirror neuron activity during observation of unpredictable grasping movements. Eur J Neurosci 20: 2193– 2202.

Goldman AI, Sripada CS (2004) Simulationist models of face-based emotion recognition. Cognition 94: 193–213.

Grèzes J, Costes N, Decety J (1998) Top-down effect of strategy on the perception of human biological motion: a PET investigation. Cogn Neuropsychol 15: 553–582.

Grèzes J, Armony JL, Rowe J, Passingham RE (2003) Activations related to "mirror" and "canonical" neurones in the human brain: an fMRI study. Neuroimage 18: 928–937.

Gross CG, Rocha-Miranda CE, Bender DB (1972) Visual properties of neurons in the inferotemporal cortex of the macaque. J Neurophysiol 35: 96–111.

Hari R, Forss N, Avikainen S, Kirveskari S, Salenius S, Rizzolatti G (1998) Activation of human primary motor cortex during action observation: a neuromagnetic study. Proc. Natl Acad Sci USA 95: 15061–15065.

Hall, Daniel, Keith Meador, and Harold Koenig. "Measuring Religiousness in Health Research: Review and Critique." Journal of Religion and Health 47, no. 2 (2008)

Harris, Sam, Jonas Kaplan, Ashley Curiel, Susan Bookheimer, Marco

Iacoboni, and Mark Cohen. "The Neural Correlates of Religious and Nonreligious Belief." PLoS One 4, no. 10 (October 1, 2009)

Halgren, E. (1992), 'Emotional neurophysiology of the amygdala within the context of human cognition', in The Amygdala: Neurobiological Aspects of Emotion, Memory and Mental Dysfunction, ed J.P. Aggleton (New York: Wiley-Liss).

Halligan PW, Fink GR, Marshal JC, Vallar G. 2003. Spatial cognition: evidence from visual neglect. Trends Cogn Sci.

Handbook of Emotions, Edited by Michael Lewis, Jeannette M. Haviland-Jones, and Lisa Feldman Barrett, The Guilford Press; 3rd edition (2010).

Haggard, P., Clark, S. and Kalogeras,]. (2002) Voluntary action and conscious awareness, Nature Neuroscience 5, 382-5. Haggard, P., Newman, C. and

Magno, E. (1999) On the perceived time of voluntary actions. British Journal of Psychology 90, 291-303.

Hameroff, S.R. and Penrose, R. (1996) Conscious events as orchestrated space-time selections. Journal of Consciousness Studies 3(1), 36-53; also reprinted in J. Shear (ed.) (1997) Explaining Consciousness-The Hard Problem. Cambridge, MA, MIT Press, 177-95.

Hardcastle, V.G. (2000) How to understand theN in NCC. InT. Metzinger (ed.) Neural Correlates of Consciousness. Cambridge, MA, MIT Press, 259-64.

Harding, D.E. (1961) On Having no Head: Zen and the Re-Discovery of the Obvious. London, Buddhist Society.

Hardy, A. (1979) The Spiritual Nature of Man: A Study of Contemporary Religious Experience. Oxford, Clarendon Press.

Hamad, S. (1990) The symbol grounding problem. Physica D 42, 335-46.

Hamad, S. (2001) No easy way out. The Sciences 41(2), 36-42.

Harre, R. and Gillett, G. (1994) The Discursive Mind. Thousand Oaks, CA, Sage.

Haugeland, J. (ed.) (1997) Mind Design II: Philosophy, Psychology, Artificial Intelligence. Cambridge, MA, MIT Press.

Hauser, M.D. (2000) Wild Minds: What Animals Really Think. New York, Henry Holt and Co.; London, Penguin.

Hearne, K. (1990) The Dream Machine. Northants, Aquarian.

Hebb, D.O. (1949) The Organization of Behavior. New York, Wiley.

Helmholtz, H.L.F. von (1856-67) Treatise on Physiological Optics.

Heyes, C.M. (1998) Theory of mind in nonhuman primates. Behavioral and Brain Sciences 21, 101-48; with commentaries.

Heyes, C.M. and Galef, B.G. (eds) (1996) Social Learning in Animals: The Roots of Culture. San Diego, CA, Academic Press.

Hilgard, E.R. (1986) Divided Consciousness: Multiple Controls in Human Thought and Action. New York, Wiley.

Hocquette JF (2016) Is in vitro meat the

solution for the future? Meat Science 120:

167–176

Hodgson, R. (1891) A case of double consciousness. Proceedings of the Society for Psychical Research 7, 221-58.

Hofstadter, D.R. (1979) Code!, Escher, Bach: An Eternal Golden Braid. London, Penguin.

Hofstadter, D.R. and Dennett, D.C. (eds) (1981) The Mind's I: Fantasies and Reflections on Self and Soul. London, Penguin.

Holland, J. (ed.) (2001) Ecstasy: The Complete Guide: A Comprehensive Look at the Risks and Benefits of MDMA. Rochester, VT, Park Street Press.

Holmes, D.S. (1987) The influence of meditation versus rest on physiological arousal. In M. West (ed.) The Psychology of Meditation. Oxford, Clarendon Press, 81-103.

Holt, J. (1999) Blindsight in debates about qualia. Journal of Consciousness Studies 6(5), 54-71.

Horgan, J. (1994), 'Can science explain consciousness?', Scientific American, 271.

Holloway RL (1996) Evolution of the human brain. In: Lock A, Peters CR (eds) Handbook of human symbolic evolution. Oxford University Press, Oxford

Iacoboni M, Woods RP, Brass M, Bekkering H, Mazziotta JC, Rizzolatti G (1999) Cortical mechanisms of human imitation. Science 286: 2526–2528.

Iacoboni M, Koski LM, Brass M, Bekkering H, Woods RP, Dubeau MC, Mazziotta JC, Rizzolatti G (2001) Reafferent copies of imitated actions in the right superior temporal cortex. Proc Natl Acad Sci USA 98: 13995–13999.

Jeannerod M (1988) The neural and behavioural organization of goal-directed movements. Clarendon Press, Oxford.

Johnson-Frey SH, Maloof FR, Newman-Norlund R, Farrer C, Inati S,

Grafton ST (2003) Actions or hand-objects interactions? Human inferior frontal cortex and action observation. Neuron 39: 1053–1058.

Jackson, F. (1982) Epiphenomenal qualia. Philosophical Quarterly 32, 127-36.

James, W. (1890) The Principles of Psychology (2 volumes). London, Macmillan.

James, W. (1902) The Varieties of Religious Experience: A Study in Human Nature. New York and London, Longmans, Green and Co.

Jansen, K. (2001) Ketamine: Dreams and Realities. Sarasota, FL, Multidisciplinary Association for Psychedelic Studies.

Jay, M. (ed.) (1999) Artificial Paradises: A Drugs Reader. London, Penguin.

Jaynes, J. (1976) The Origin of Consciousness in the Breakdown of the Bicameral Mind. New York, Houghton Mifflin.

Johnson, M.K. and Raye, C.L. (1981) Reality monitoring. Psychological Review 88, 67-85.

Kadim I, Mahgoub O, Baqir S et al. (2015) Cultured meat from muscle stem cells: a review of challenges and prospects. J Integr Agr 14: 222–233

Koski L, Iacoboni M, Dubeau MC, Woods RP, Mazziotta JC (2003) Modulation of cortical activity during different imitative behaviors. J Neurophysiol 89: 460–471.

Krolak-Salmon P, Henaff MA, Isnard J, Tallon-Baudry C, Guenot M, Vighetto A, Bertrand O, Mauguiere F (2003) An attention modulated response to disgust in human ventral anterior insula. Ann Neurol 53: 446–453.

Kandel, E. R. In Search of Memory: The Emergence of a New Science of

Mind, W. W. Norton & Company (2007).

Kandel E. R. Schwartz JH, Jessel TM. Principles of neural sciences. New York; McGraw Hill, 2000.

Kanizsa, G. (1979), Organization In Vision (New York: Praeger).

Kaloupek DG, Scott JR, Khatami V. Assessment of coping strategies associated with syncope in blood donors. J Psychosom Res. 1985;29:207-214.

Kanwisher, N. (2001) Neural events and perceptual awareness. Cognition 79, 89-113; also reprinted inS. Dehaene (ed.) The Cognitive Neuroscience of Consciousness. Cambridge, MA, MIT Press, 89-113.

Kapleau, Roshi P. (1980) The Three Pillars of Zen: Teaching, Practice, and Enlightenment (revised edn). New York, Doubleday.

Karn, K. and Hayhoe, M. (2000) Memory representations guide targeting eye movements in a natural task. Visual Cognition 7, 673-703.

Kasamatsu, A. and Hirai, T. (1966) An electroencephalographic study on the Zen meditation (zazen). Folia Psychiatrica et Neurologica Japonica 20, 315-36.

Kaiserman-Abramof, I. R., Graybiel, A. M., & Nauta, W. J. (1980). The thalamic projection to cortical area 17 in a congenitally anophthalmic mouse strain. Neuroscience, 5, 41–52.

Kanold, P. O., Kara, P., Reid, R. C., & Shatz, C. J. (2003). Role of subplate neurons in functional maturation of visual cortical columns. Science, 301, 521–525.

Kennedy, H., & Dehay, C. (1988). Functional implications of the anatomical organization of the callosal projections of visual areas V1 and V2 in the macaque monkey. Behav. Brain Res., 29, 225–236.

Kennedy, H., & Dehay, C. (1993). Cortical specifi cation of mice and men. Cereb. Cortex, 3, 171–186.

Kentridge, R.W. and Heywood, C.A. (1999) The status of blindsight. Journal of Consciousness Studies 6(5), 3-11.

Kihlstrom, J.F. (1996) Perception without awareness of what is perceived, learning without awareness of what is learned. In M. Velmans (ed.) The Science of Consciousness. London, Routledge, 23-46.

Kluver, H. (1926) Mescal visions and eidetic vision. American Journal of Psychology 37, 502-15.

Kollerstrom, N. (1999) The path of Halley's comet, and Newton's late apprehension of the law of gravity. Annals of Science 56, 331-56.

Kosslyn, S.M. (1980) Image and Mind. Cambridge, MA, Harvard University Press.

Kosslyn, S.M. (1988) Aspects of a cognitive neuroscience of mental imagery. Science 240, 1621-6.

Kinsbourne, M. (1995), 'The intralaminar thalamic nucleii', Consciousness and Cognition, 4.

Kjaer, Troels, Camilla Bertelsen, Paola Piccini, David Brooks, Jorgen Alving, and Hans Lou. "Increased Dopamine Tone during Meditation- Induced Change of Consciousness." Cognitive Brain Research 13, no. 2 (April 2002)

Kölmel HW. 1985. Complex visual hallucinations in the hemianopic field. J Neurol Neurosurg Psychiatry.

Koenig, Harold. "Research on Religion, Spirituality, and Mental Health: A Review." Canadian Journal of Psychiatry 54, no. 5 (May 2009)

Koenig, Harold, ed. Handbook of Religion and Mental Health. San Diego, CA: Academic Press, 1998

Kraepelin E. Psychiatry: A Textbook for Students and Physicians. New York, NY: Science History Publications; 1990.

Lauglin, Charles, John McManus, and Eugene d'Aquili. Brain, Symbol, and Experience. 2nd ed. New York: Columbia University Press, 1992

Lakoff, G. and M. Johnson (1999). Philosophy in the flesh. Basic Books: New York.

LeDoux, J. E. (1996). The emotional brain. New York: Simon & Schuster.

LeDoux, J.E. (1992), 'Emotion and the amygdala', in The Amygdala: Neurobiological Aspects of Emo- tion, Memory and Mental Dysfunction, ed J.P. Aggleton (New York: Wiley-Liss).

Levin, D.T. and Simons, D.J. (1997) Failure to detect changes to attended objects in motion pictures. Psychonomic Bulletin and Review 4, 501-6.

Levine,J. (1983) Materialism and qualia: the explanatory gap. Pacific Philosophical Quarterly 64, 354-61.

Levine,J. (2001) Purple Haze: The Puzzle of Consciousness. New York, Oxford University Press. Levine, S. (1979) A Gradual Awakening. New York, Doubleday.

Levinson, B.W. (1965) States of awareness during general anaesthesia. British Journal of Anaesthesia 37, 544-6.

Lewicki, P., Czyzewska, M. and Hoffman, H. (1987) Unconscious acquisition of complex procedural knowledge. Journal of Experimental Psychology: Learning, Memory and Cognition 13, 523-30.

Lewicki, P., Hill, T. and Bizot, E. (1988) Acquisition of procedural knowledge about a pattern of stimuli that cannot be articulated. Cognitive Psychology 20, 24-37.

Lewicki, P., Hill, T. and Czyzewska, M. (1992) Nonconscious acquisition of information. American Psychologist 47, 796-801.

Manthey S, Schubotz RI, von Cramon DY (2003). Premotor cortex in observing erroneous action: an fMRI study. Brain Res Cogn Brain Res 15: 296–307.

M. Colombo, "Why build a virtual brain? Large-scale neural simulations as jump start for cognitive computing," Journal of Experimental and Theoretical Artificial Intelligence, vol. 29, pp. 361-370, 2017.

Mesulam MM, Mufson EJ (1982) Insula of the old world monkey. III: Efferent cortical output and comments on function. J Comp Neurol 212: 38–52.

Naskar, Abhijit. "What is Mind?", 2016

Naskar, Abhijit. "In Search of Divinity: Journey to The Kingdom of Conscience", 2016

Naskar, Abhijit. "Love, God & Neurons: Memoir of A Scientist who found himself by getting lost", 2016

Naskar, Abhijit. "Neurons of Jesus: Mind of A Teacher, Spouse & Thinker", 2017

Naskar, Abhijit. "Rowdy Buddha: The First Sapiens", 2017

Naskar, Abhijit. "The Education Decree", 2017

Naskar, Abhijit. "Principia Humanitas", 2017

Naskar, Abhijit. "We Are All Black: A Treatise on Racism", 2017

Naskar, Abhijit. "Wise Mating: A Treatise on Monogamy", 2017

Naskar, Abhijit. "Illusion of Religion: A Treatise on Religious Fundamentalism", 2017

Naskar, Abhijit. "I Am The Thread: My Mission", 2017

Naskar, Abhijit. "Morality Absolute", 2017

Naskar, Abhijit. "Fabric of Humanity", 2018

Naskar, Abhijit. "The Constitution of The United Peoples of Earth", 2019

Naskar, Abhijit. "When Humans Unite: Making A World Without Borders", 2019

Naskar, Abhijit. "Mission Reality", 2019

Naskar, Abhijit. "On the Nature of Democratic Psychology". EC Psychology and Psychiatry 7.6, 335-337. (2018)

Newberg, Andrew, and Jeremy Iversen. "The Neural Basis of the Complex Mental Task of Meditation: Neurotransmitter and Neurochemical Considerations." Medical Hypotheses 61, no. 2 (2003).

Newberg, Andrew. "How God Changes Your Brain: An Introduction to Jewish Neurotheology", CCAR Journal: The Reform Jewish Quarterly, Winter 2016.

Newberg, Andrew, and Stephanie Newberg. "A Neuropsychological Perspective on Spiritual Development." In Handbook of Spiritual Development in Childhood and Adolescence, edited by Eugene Roehlkepartain, Pamela King, Linda Wagener, and Peter Benson. London: Sage Publications, Inc., 2005

Newberg, Andrew. "The Neurotheology Link An Intersection Between Spirituality and Health",

Alternative and Complimentary Therapies, Vol 21 No 1, February 2015.

Newberg, Andrew, Nancy Wintering, Dharma Khalsa, Hannah Roggenkamp, and Mark Waldman. "Meditation Effects on Cognitive Function and Cerebral Blood Flow in Subjects with Memory Loss: A Preliminary Study." Journal of Alzheimer's Disease 20, no. 2 (2010)

Nash, M. (1995), 'Glimpses of the mind', Time.

Nesse RM. Proximate and evolutionary studies of anxiety, stress and depression: synergy at the interface. Neurosci Biobehav Rev. 1999;23:895-903.

Nishitani N, Hari R (2000) Temporal dynamics of cortical representation for action. Proc Natl Acad Sci USA 97: 913–918.

Nishitani N, Hari R (2002) Viewing lip forms: cortical dynamics. Neuron 36: 1211–1220.

O'Hara, K. and Scutt, T. (1996) There is no hard problem of consciousness. Journal of Consciousness Studies 3(4), 290-302, reprinted in J. Shear (ed.) (1997) Explaining Consciousness. Cambridge, MA, MIT Press, 69-82.

O'Regan, J.K. (1992) Solving the "real" mysteries of visual perception: the world as an outside memory. Canadian Journal of Psychology 46, 461-88.

O'Regan, J.K. and Noe, A. (2001) A sensorimotor account of vision and visual consciousness. Behavioral and Brain Sciences 24(5), 883-917.

O'Regan, J.K., Rensink, R.A. and Clark,].]. (1999) Change-blindness as a result of "mudsplashes." Nature 398, 34.

Ornstein, R.E. (1977) The Psychology of Consciousness (2nd edn). New York, Harcourt.

Ornstein, R.E. (1986) The Psychology of Consciousness (3rd edn). New York, Pehguin.

Ornstein, R.E. (1992) The Evolution of Consciousness. New York, Touchstone.

Penfield W, Faulk ME (1955) The insula: further observations on its function. Brain 78: 445– 470.

Penrose, R. (1994), Shadows of the Mind (Oxford: Oxford University Press).

Penrose, R. (1989), The Emperor's New Mind: Concerning Computers, Minds and The Laws of Physics (Oxford: Oxford University Press).

Persinger, "'I would kill in God's name' role of sex, weekly church attendance, report of a religious experience and limbic lability" Perceptual and Motor Skills 1997.

Persinger "Experimental simulation of the God experience" Neurotheology 2003.

Persinger, M. A. (1993b). Personality changes following brain injury as a grief response to the loss of sense of self: Phenomenological themes as indices of local lability and neurocognitive restructuring as psycho- therapy. Psychological Reports, 72

Persinger, Corradini, Clement, Keaney, et al "Neurotheology and its convergence with neuroquantology" NeuroQuantology 2010.

Persinger, Koren and St-Pierre "The electromagnetic induction of mystical and altered states within the laboratory" Journal of Consciousness Exploration and Research 2010.

Persinger "Case report: A prototypical spontaneous 'sensed presence' of a sentient being and concomitant electroencephalographic activity in the clinical laboratory" Neurocase 2008.

Persinger and Saroka "Potential production of Hughlings Jackson's "parasitic consciousness" by physiologically-patterned weak transcerebral magnetic fields: QEEG and source localization" Epilepsy & Behavior 28 (2013).

Persinger. "The neuropsychiatry of paranormal experiences". J Neuropsychiatry Clin Neurosci 2001.

Persinger. "Neuropsychological bases of god beliefs", New York: Praeger, 1987

Persinger. "Temporal lobe epileptic signs and correlative behaviors displayed by normal populations", Journal of General Psychology, 1986

Persinger "Experimental Facilitation of the Sensed Presence: Possible Intercalation between the Hemispheres Induced by Complex Magnetic Fields" Journal of Nervous and Mental Disease 2002.

Palmer J. 1978. The out-of-body experience: a psychological theory. Parapsychol Rev.

Page AC. Blood-injury phobia. Clinical Psychology Review. 1994;14:443-461.

Perry BD, Pollard R. Homeostasis, stress, trauma, and adaptation. A neurodevelopmental view of childhood trauma. Child Adolesc Psychiatr Clin N Am. 1998;7:33.

Paré, D. & Llinás, R. (1995), 'Conscious and preconscious processes as seen from the standpoint of sleep-waking cycle neurophysiology', Neuropsychologia, 33.

P. S. de Laplace. Essai Philosophique sur les Probabilites [1814], in Academy des Sciences, Oeuvres Complotes de Laplace, Vol. 7, Gauthier-Villars, Paris (1886).

Perrett DI, Harries MH, Bevan R, Thomas S, Benson PJ, Mistlin AJ, Chitty AJ, Hietanen JK, Ortega JE (1989) Frameworks of analysis for the neural representation of animate objects and actions. J Exp Bio 146: 87–113.

Phillips ML, Young AW, Senior C, Brammer M, Andrew C, Calder AJ, Bullmore ET, Perrett DI, Rowland D, Williams SC, Gray JA, David AS (1997) A specific neural substrate for perceiving facial expressions of disgust. Nature 389: 495–498.

Phillips ML, Young AW, Scott SK, Calder AJ, Andrew C, Giampietro V, Williams SC, Bullmore ET, Brammer M, Gray JA (1998) Neural responses to facial and vocal expressions of fear and disgust. Proc R Soc Lond B Biol Sci 265: 1809–1817.

Puce A, Perrett D (2003) Electrophysiological and brain imaging of biological motion. Philosoph Trans Royal Soc Lond, Series B, 358: 435–445.

Ramachandran VS. Behavioral and magnetoencephalographic correlates of plasticity in the adult human brain. Proc Natl Acad Sci USA 1993; 90: 10413–20.

Ramachandran VS. Phantom limbs, neglect syndromes, repressed memories, and Freudian psychology. Int Rev Neurobiol 1994; 37: 291–333.

Ramachandran VS. Plasticity and functional recovery in neurology. Clin Med 2005; 5: 368–73.

Ramachandran VS, Hirstein W. The perception of phantom limbs. The D. O. Hebb lecture. Brain 1998; 121: 1603–30.

Ramachandran VS, McGeoch PD, Williams L, Arcilla G. Rapid relief of thalamic pain syndrome induced by vestibular caloric stimulation. Neurocase 2007; 13: 185–8.

Ramachandran VS, Rogers-Ramachandran D, Cobb S. Touching the phantom limb. Nature 1995; 377: 489–90.

Ramachandran VS, Rogers-Ramachandran D. Phantom limbs and neural plasticity. Arch Neurol 2000; 57: 317–20.

Ramachandran VS, Rogers-Ramachandran D. It's all done with mirrors. Sci Am Mind 2007; 18: 16–9.

Ramachandran VS, Rogers-Ramachandran D. Sensations referred to a patient's phantom arm from another subjects intact arm: perceptual correlates of mirror neurons. Med Hypotheses 2008; 70: 1233–4.

Ramachandran VS, Rogers-Ramachandran D, Stewart M. Perceptual correlates of massive cortical reorganization. Science 1992; 258: 1159–60.

Rizzolatti G, Craighero L (2004) The mirror-neuron system. Annu Rev Neurosci 27: 169–192.

Rizzolatti G, Scandolara C, Matelli M, Gentilucci M (1981) Afferent properties of periarcuate neurons in macaque monkeys. I. Somatosensory responses. Behav Brain Res 2: 125–146.

Rizzolatti G, Fadiga L, Matelli M, Bettinardi V, Paulesu E, Perani D, Fazio F (1996) Localization of grasp representation in humans by PET: 1. Observation versus execution. Exp Brain Res 111: 246–252.

Rizzolatti G, Fogassi L, Gallese V (2001) Neurophysiological mechanisms underlying the understanding and imitation of action. Nature Rev Neurosci 2:661–670.

Rock I, Victor J. Vision and touch: an experimentally created conflict between the two senses. Science 1964; 143: 594–6.

Rose´n B, Lundborg G. Training with a mirror in rehabilitation of the hand. Scand J Plast Reconstr Surg Hand Surg 2005; 39: 104–8.

Royet JP, Plailly J, Delon-Martin C, Kareken DA, Segebarth C (2003) fMRI of emotional responses to odors: influence of hedonic valence and judgment, handedness, and gender. Neuroimage 20: 713–728.

Rozin R Haidt J and McCauley CR (2000) Disgust. In: Lewis M, Haviland-Jones JM (eds) Handbook of Emotion. 2nd Edition. Guilford Press, New York, pp 637–653.

Saxe R, Carey S, Kanwisher N (2004) Understanding other minds: linking developmental psychology and functional neuroimaging. Annu Rev Psychol 55: 87–124.

S. J. Russell and P. Norvig, Artificial intelligence: a modern approach (3rd edition): Prentice Hall, 2009.

Schienle A, Stark R, Walter B, Blecker C, Ott U, Kirsch P, Sammer G, Vaitl D (2002) The insula is not specifically involved in disgust processing: an fMRI study. Neuroreport 13: 2023–2026.

Showers MJC, Lauer EW (1961) Somatovisceral motor patterns in the insula. J Comp Neurol 117: 107–115.

Singer T, Seymour B, O'Doherty J, Kaube H, Dolan RJ, Frith CD (2004) Empathy for pain involves the affective but not the sensory components of pain. Science 303: 1157–1162.

Small DM, Gregory MD, Mak YE, Gitelman D, Mesulam MM, Parrish T (2003) Dissociation of neural representation of intensity and affective valuation in human gustation Neuron 39: 701–711.

Smith A (1759) The theory of moral sentiments (ed. 1976). Clarendon Press, Oxford.

Sprengelmeyer R, Rausch M, Eysel UT, Przuntek H (1998) Neural structures associated with recognition of facial expressions of basic emotions Proc R Soc Lond B Biol Sci 265: 1927–1931.

Strafella AP, Paus T (2000) Modulation of cortical excitability during action observation: a transcranial magnetic stimulation study. NeuroReport 11: 2289–2292.

Simonsen R (2015) Eating for the future: veganism and the challenge of in vitro meat. In: Stapleton P, Byers A (Hg). Biopolitics and utopia. Palgrave Macmillan, New York (2015), S 167–190

Tanaka K (1996) Inferotemporal cortex and object vision. Ann Rev Neurosci. 19: 109–140.

T. R. Society, "Machine learning: the power and promise of computers that learn by example," ed. The Royal Society, 2017.

Tomasello M, Call J (1997) Primate cognition. Oxford University Press, Oxford.

Tremblay C, Robert M, Pascual-Leone A, Lepore F, Nguyen DK, Carmant L, Bouthillier A, Theoret H (2004) Action observation and execution: intracranial recordings in a human subject. Neurology. 63: 937–938.

Umilta MA, Kohler E, Gallese V, Fogassi L, Fadiga L, Keysers C, Rizzolatti G (2001) "I know what you are doing": a neurophysiological study. Neuron 32: 91–101.

Von Wright G.H., (1963), Norm and Action. A Logical Inquiry, Routledge & Kegan Paul, London.

Von Wright G.H., (1976), "Determinism and the Study of Man", in Essays on Explanation and Understanding, ed. by J. Manninen and R. Tuomela, Reidel, Dordrecht.

Von Wright G.H., (1977), "What is Humanism?", The Lindlay Lecture, University of Arkansas, Lawrence, Kansas.

Von Wright G.H., (1979), "Humanism and the Humanities", in Philosophy and Grammar, ed. by S. Kanger and S. Öhman, Reidel, Dordrecht, pp. 1-16. Reprinted in von Wright (1993).

Von Wright G.H., (1980), Freedom and Determination, North-Holland Publishing Co., Amsterdam.

Von Wright G.H., (1985), Of Human Freedom, The Tanner Lectures on Human Values,

Vol. VI, ed. by S. M. McMurrin, University of Utah Press, Salt Lake City, pp. 107-70. Reprinted in von Wright (1998).

Von Wright G.H., (1993), The Tree of Knowledge and Other Essays, Brill, Leiden.

Von Wright G.H., (1997), "Progress: Fact and Fiction", in The Idea of Progress, ed. by A. Burgen et al., W. de Gruyter, Berlin, pp. 1-18.

Von Wright G.H., (1998), In the Shadow of Descartes: Essays in the Philosophy of Mind, Kluwer, Dordrecht.

Visalberghi E, Fragaszy D. (2002). Do monkeys ape? Ten years after. In: Dautenhahn K, Nehaniv C (eds) Imitation in animals and artifacts. MIT Press, Boston. Pp. 471–500

Weele C, Driessen C. (2016) In vitro meat is a chance to rethink. In: Stephens N, Kramer C, Denfeld Z,

Strand R (Hg). What is in vitro meat? Food Phreaking Issue 02: 57–59

Wicker B, Keysers C, Plailly J, Royet JP, Gallese V, Rizzolatti G (2003) Both of us disgusted in my insula: the common neural basis of seeing and feeling disgust. Neuron 40: 655–664.

Yokochi H, Tanaka M, Kumashiro M, Iriki A (2003) Inferior parietal somatosensory neurons coding face-hand coordination in Japanese macaques. Somatosens Mot Res 20 : 115–125.

Zald DH, Pardo JV (2000) Functional neuroimaging of the olfactory system in humans. Int J Psychophysiol 36: 165–181.

Zald DH, Donndelinger MJ, Pardo JV (1998) Elucidating dynamic brain interactions with across-subjects correlational analyses of positron emission tomographic data: the functional connectivity of the amygdala and orbitofrontal cortex during olfactory tasks. J Cereb Blood Flow Metab 18: 896–905.

127

129

131

133

www.ingramcontent.com/pod-product-compliance
Lightning Source LLC
Chambersburg PA
CBHW051457250726
48655CB00001B/461